UNDERGROUND TRANSPORTATION SYSTEMS

Simon Rose

CRABTREE
PUBLISHING COMPANY
WWW.CRABTREEBOOKS.COM

Author: Simon Rose

Editorial Director: Kathy Middleton

Editors: Petrice Custance, Sonya Newland

Proofreaders: Lorna Notsch, Ellen Rodger

Designer: Steve Mead

Cover design: Tammy McGarr

**Production coordinator and
    Prepress technician:** Tammy McGarr

Print coordinator: Katherine Berti

Produced for Crabtree Publishing Company
by White-Thomson Publishing Ltd

Photographs

Cover: Shutterstock: ©Marco Rubino (left); ©PI (right middle);
All other images from Shutterstock

Interior: Alamy: 8–9 (Guy Corbishley), 11b (Elizabeth Wake), 17 (Felix
Lipov), 20 (Endless Travel), 21 (Military History Collection), 23 (Michael
Dwyer); Julian Baker: 19, 22–23, 28; Getty Images: 5 (Boston Globe), 6–7
(Print Collector), 7 (Science & Society Picture Library), 8 (Bettmann), 11t
(PhotoQuest), 12–13 (Spencer Platt), 16 (Cincinnati Museum Center), 18b
(Glyn Kirk), 25 (KRISTOF VAN ACCOM), 26–27 (Photo 12), 27 (AFP);
iStock: 12 (Apitch), 14 (finallast); Shutterstock: 4–5 (Lux Blue), 10 (Everett
Historical), 15t (Marco Rubino), 15b (Arthit Kaeoratanapattama), 18t
(Filip Fuxa), 24 (SCK_Photo), 29 (HildaWeges Photography).

Library and Archives Canada Cataloguing in Publication

Rose, Simon, 1961-, author
        Underground transportation systems / Simon Rose.

(Underground worlds)
Includes index.
Issued in print and electronic formats.
ISBN 978-0-7787-6127-3 (hardcover).--
ISBN 978-0-7787-6165-5 (softcover).--
ISBN 978-1-4271-2252-0 (HTML)

        1. Subways--Juvenile literature. 2. Tunnels--Juvenile literature.
3. Underground construction--Juvenile literature. I. Title.

TF845.R67 2018   j388.4'2   C2018-905532-4
                                          C2018-905533-2

Library of Congress Cataloging-in-Publication Data

Names: Rose, Simon, 1961- author.
Title: Underground transportation systems / Simon Rose.
Description: New York, New York : Crabtree Publishing Company, [2019]
    | Series: Underground worlds | Includes index.
Identifiers: LCCN 2018043800 (print) | LCCN 2018049449 (ebook) |
    ISBN 9781427122520 (Electronic) |
    ISBN 9780778761273 (hardcover) |
    ISBN 9780778761655 (pbk.)
Subjects: LCSH: Tunnels--Transportation--Juvenile literature. |
    Subways--Juvenile literature. | Underground construction--Juvenile
    literature. | CYAC: Tunnels. | Subways. | Underground construction. |
    LCGFT: Instructional and educational works.
Classification: LCC TA807 (ebook) | LCC TA807 .R67 2019 (print) |
    DDC 388.4/2--dc23
LC record available at https://lccn.loc.gov/2018043800

Crabtree Publishing Company

www.crabtreebooks.com   1-800-387-7650

Printed in the U.S.A./122018/CG20181005

Published in Canada
Crabtree Publishing
616 Welland Ave.
St. Catharines, Ontario
L2M 5V6

Published in the United States
Crabtree Publishing
PMB 59051
350 Fifth Avenue, 59th Floor
New York, New York 10118

Published in the United Kingdom
Crabtree Publishing
Maritime House
Basin Road North, Hove
BN41 1WR

Published in Australia
Crabtree Publishing
3 Charles Street
Coburg North
VIC, 3058

CONTENTS

GETTING AROUND UNDERGROUND 4

THE LONDON UNDERGROUND 6

THE NEW YORK CITY SUBWAY 10

THE MOSCOW METRO 14

ABANDONED SUBWAY SYSTEMS 16

ESCAPE TUNNELS 18

THE GIBRALTAR TUNNELS 20

UNDERGROUND ROADS AND HIGHWAYS 22

BELOW LAND AND WATER 24

MINING TUNNELS 26

THE CHANNEL TUNNEL 28

GLOSSARY 30

LEARNING MORE 31

INDEX 32

GETTING AROUND UNDERGROUND

About 200 years ago, cities began to grow dramatically. As more and more people crowded into them, transportation became a problem. **Navigating** through city streets became difficult due to **congestion**. The solution? Go underground!

Trains under the Earth

There are around 160 underground rail systems in large cities around the world. They are known by different names, including subway, metro, and the underground. Underground railways run under city streets, buildings, and even rivers.

Underground rail tracks are usually designed to match the **gauge** of the rest of the city's train system. This means that underground trains can connect seamlessly with aboveground networks. The trains are powered by electricity from overhead cables or from an electrified third rail, which lies either between or at the side of the other two rails.

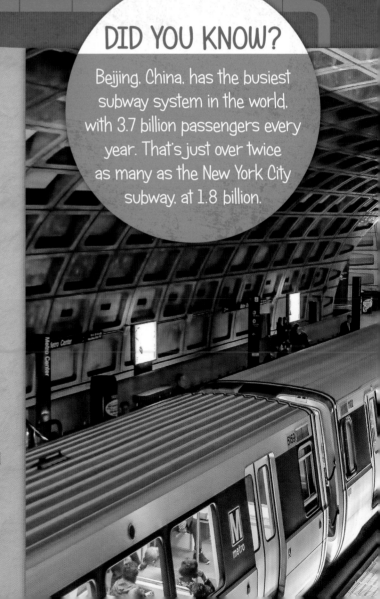

DID YOU KNOW?

Beijing, China, has the busiest subway system in the world, with 3.7 billion passengers every year. That's just over twice as many as the New York City subway, at 1.8 billion.

Roads and Tunnels

Subway trains aren't the only things that travel underground. There are also underground transportation systems for road vehicles, and trains that travel beneath mountains or under the sea. There are even tunnels used for mining operations, to move people and equipment around underground.

▽ The Big Dig in Boston (see page 22) is a 7.8-mile (12.6-km) underground highway.

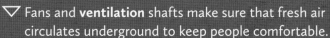

▽ Fans and **ventilation** shafts make sure that fresh air circulates underground to keep people comfortable.

Secret Passages

Some tunnels were built in great secrecy. These were often dug in wartime for defense or as headquarters for important people. Others were built so that soldiers could move around in secret and make surprise attacks. Some tunnels were dug by prisoners of war, desperate to escape.

THE LONDON UNDERGROUND

In London in the 1800s, transportation options were to walk or take a horse-drawn carriage. This meant that people had to live close to where they worked, which led to overcrowding in certain parts of the city.

Breaking Ground

To provide cheap, fast transportation, it was decided to build a rail system below London's busy streets. Few machines were available in those days, so workers had to dig by hand using picks and shovels. They started by digging a large, deep trench. From there, tracks and tunnels were built. As workers carved out each tunnel, others followed behind them, lining it with bricks. This strengthened it and held back the earth.

The First Underground Railway

The first line was the Metropolitan Line, which ran 4 miles (6 km) between Paddington in the west and Farringdon in the east. The grand opening took place on January 9, 1863, when around 40,000 people journeyed on this **pioneering** rail system. Early trains on the London Underground ran on steam from burning coal, so there was a lot of smoke in tunnels and stations. By 1913, however, the whole system had switched to electric power.

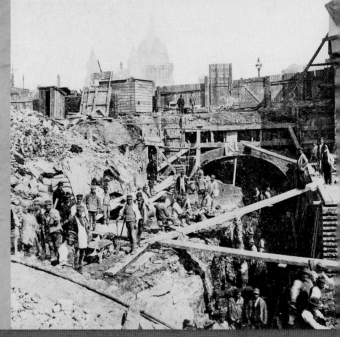

△ Digging was a long, hard job. Sometimes only 4 inches (10 cm) of tunnel were dug in one whole day.

DID YOU KNOW?

Around 55 percent of the London Underground is actually aboveground!

◁ Opened in 1843, the Thames Tunnel was one of the earliest transportation tunnels in London. It was designed for carriages to travel beneath the River Thames, which flows through London.

Hiding Underground

During World War II (1939–45), Germany launched nighttime bomb attacks on London. Many Underground stations were used as shelters from **air raids**. But the Underground was not always safe. In 1943, 173 people were killed in a crush on a crowded staircase at Bethnal Green Station. Throughout the war, about 200 people were killed when different stations took direct bomb hits.

△ During World War II, people slept on the platforms—and sometimes even on the tracks.

DID YOU KNOW?

In the early 1900s, traveling on the Underground cost two pennies. This earned it the nickname the "Twopenny Tube." Londoners still refer to it as the "Tube."

△ Tunneling today is very different from the early days. The latest technology is being used to build the Elizabeth Line.

The Future

Today, an average of 2.7 million journeys are made on the London Underground every day. It has 270 stations, linked by 249 miles (402 km) of rail lines. And it is still growing! The latest line to be built is the Elizabeth Line, which is due to open in 2019. Running across London from east to west, the Elizabeth Line will connect 26 miles (41.8 km) of new tunnels to 30 existing Underground stations.

THE NEW YORK CITY SUBWAY

In 1888, New York was hit by the Great Blizzard. This was a huge storm that caused severe damage and killed more than 400 people. Officials realized that an underground transportation system was needed in the city to make travel safer during the winter months.

A Dangerous Job

Construction on the New York City Subway began in 1900. Around 8,000 workers were employed for this backbreaking job. They tunneled by hand—and it was dangerous work. There was always the risk of rockfalls or a tunnel collapsing. Thousands were injured, and more than 60 men died during construction.

▽ These workers are drilling in the tunnels during the construction of the subway system.

A Nickel to Ride

The subway opened on October 27, 1904. New York mayor George McClelland drove the first train from City Hall to 103rd Street. When the subway opened to the public that evening, more than 100,000 people each paid a nickel to take their first ride beneath Manhattan. The first line ran 9.1 miles (14.6 km) through 28 stations.

The system was expanded to the Bronx in 1905, Brooklyn in 1908, and Queens in 1915. Three years later, the system's worst accident happened. A train driver lost control entering a tunnel in Brooklyn. More than 200 people were injured and 97 died.

△ City officials opened the first line in 1904.

DID YOU KNOW?

Local artists have sometimes created artwork for New York's subway stations. At the 14th Street/Eighth Avenue Station, there are more than 130 bronze **sculptures**, including one of an alligator emerging from a manhole cover!

11

Turnstiles and Tokens

Subway travelers bought tickets to ride on the subway until 1920, when **turnstiles** were introduced. These first accepted nickels and then dimes. Then in 1953, subway **tokens** were introduced. These were used for 50 years—until 2003. Today, people use a MetroCard. This can be loaded with train fares, then swiped at the station turnstiles.

▽ Construction of the Second Avenue Subway began in 2007. The first phase was completed 10 years later.

◁ A green lamp at a station entrance means that it is always open. A red light means that the station is only open some of the time.

The System Today

Today, the New York City Subway is one of the world's busiest underground transportation systems. Every weekday, around 5.6 million passengers take the subway. The system has 468 stations and 26 lines. In Manhattan, the system's trains mostly run underground. In other areas of New York City, however, many trains run on elevated tracks. In fact, 40 percent of the New York transit system is aboveground.

DID YOU KNOW?

Between 2001 and 2010, 2,500 old New York City subway cars were sunk into the Atlantic Ocean. They are used as **artificial reefs** and are now home to many types of marine life.

13

THE MOSCOW METRO

In January 1931, a huge traffic jam in Moscow brought vehicles in the city to a halt. Officials decided to solve the congestion problem by building an underground rail network.

Construction Problems

To begin with, the digging was very difficult. Tunnelers had to deal with different types of soil, limestone rock, quicksand, and underground rivers. In 1934, a special machine called a tunneling shield was brought in from Britain. This was a temporary structure that supported the walls and ceiling so they would not collapse. The speed of work improved dramatically, and the Moscow Metro—complete with 13 stations—opened in 1935.

Revolution and War

During World War II, Mayakovskaya Station was used as a bomb shelter, a hospital, and as the headquarters of the country's military command. In 1941, Soviet leader Joseph Stalin celebrated the anniversary of the **Russian Revolution** at this station.

▽ Events from the Russian Revolution are shown in the **mosaics** displayed in Mayakovskaya Station.

△ Ploshchad Revolyutsii subway station has many bronze sculptures of ordinary Russian people.

People's Palaces

Several stations double as museums of Russian history, with many statues and paintings. The stations were designed to be underground "palaces of the people." Komsomolskaya Station has high ceilings and chandeliers. In Novokuznetskaya Station, there are carvings, bronze statues of war heroes, and seven ceiling mosaics. Novoslobodskaya Station has 32 stained-glass panels with brass borders.

DID YOU KNOW?

At Ploshchad Revolyutsii Station, some believe that rubbing the nose of a bronze dog statue will bring good luck.

ABANDONED SUBWAY SYSTEMS

In some cities, there are ghostly abandoned tunnels deep below the streets. Some places have stations or entire systems that were never completed or were closed down after being used for some time.

The Cincinnati Subway

At 2.2 miles (3.5 km) long, the Cincinnati Subway is the largest abandoned subway system in the United States. The main tunnel was built in the early 1920s, but work halted in 1927 after the **investors** stopped funding the project. No tracks were ever put into the tunnels, and the city authorities did not order any train cars. Six stations were built but were never used. For many years, tours could be taken through the long-abandoned tunnels. Now they are considered unsafe and are closed to the public.

▽ Only a small section of the planned 16-mile (26-km) Cincinnati system was completed.

Presidential Platform

New York is also home to several abandoned subway stations. Some of these were originally owned by private companies. They were closed in 1940, when the City of New York took over the lines. One of the most famous is the Track 61 platform, which lies beneath the Waldorf Astoria Hotel in New York City. Although abandoned, it is rumored that presidents still use this track to get into and out of the city in secret. President Franklin D. Roosevelt used it when he visited New York during World War II.

DID YOU KNOW?

Aldwych Underground Station in London closed in 1994, but is often used as a location for filming movies and TV shows.

▽ The train Roosevelt used stands abandoned by the disused Waldorf Astoria platform.

X498

ESCAPE TUNNELS

Sometimes, underground tunnels are built in desperate times so that people can hide or escape. In wartime, tunnels were built so that soldiers could travel in secret.

Secret Tunnels

Tunnels were included when Dover Castle was built in Britain in the **Middle Ages**. They allowed soldiers to move around without being seen by the enemy. Over the centuries, more tunnels were added. During World War II, they were used as a military command center for the army, navy, and air force. There was also an underground hospital; accommodation for soldiers, kitchens, offices; and a telephone system.

Guard tower

Exit shaft

The escape tunnel ▷ at Stalag Luft III

▽ A wartime operations room in the tunnels beneath Dover Castle.

Digging to Freedom

During World War II, **Allied** soldiers dug tunnels to escape from a German prison camp called Stalag Luft III. The tunnel, which the prisoners named "Harry," was 360 feet (110 m) long. It ran from the **barracks** and under the camp's fence, emerging near some woods. The prisoners made digging tools from milk cans. They put the dug-out soil in small pouches made from old socks, then emptied these out when they were allowed to exercise in the prison yard. They used boards from their beds to strengthen the tunnel and hold back soil. In March 1944, 76 men escaped through the tunnel, but only three reached safety—the rest were caught.

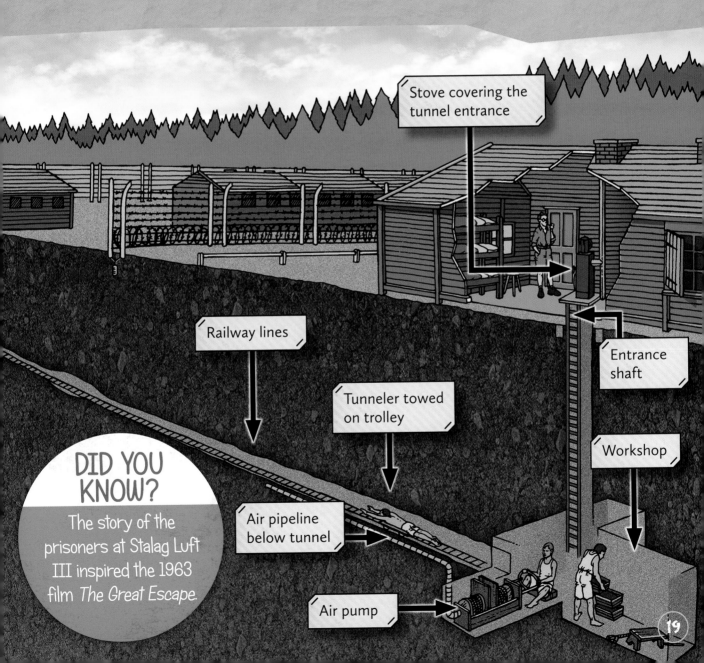

Stove covering the tunnel entrance

Railway lines

Entrance shaft

Tunneler towed on trolley

Workshop

Air pipeline below tunnel

Air pump

DID YOU KNOW?

The story of the prisoners at Stalag Luft III inspired the 1963 film *The Great Escape.*

THE GIBRALTAR TUNNELS

Gibraltar is a British territory near the south of Spain, at the entrance to the Mediterranean Sea. Deep within the famous **Rock of Gibraltar** is a whole network of secret tunnels.

The Great Siege Tunnels

The tunnels were built by the British Army over the course of about 200 years. The Great **Siege** Tunnels were begun in 1779, when Britain was at war with France and Spain and the Rock came under siege. The tunnels took four years to build, with workers using heavy hammers, crowbars, and gunpowder to blast away the rock. When the work was completed, cannons were placed in openings so that British soldiers could fire at the enemy from the safety of this retreat.

△ The total length of the tunnel network inside the Rock is around 34 miles (52 km).

The Tunnels in World War II

During World War II, the British were worried that the Germans would attack Gibraltar. They decided to turn the Rock into an underground fortress where around 16,000 soldiers with weapons, equipment, supplies, and ammunition could survive a long enemy siege. They built a power station, telephone system, hospital, bakery, laundry, and toilet facilities. There was enough food to last for 16 months.

DID YOU KNOW?

The Stay Behind Cave was a last retreat if the Rock was captured. Soldiers would be able to report on movements of enemy ships from this hiding place. Six men could have stayed in the space for around a year.

▽ British Royal Engineers and soldiers from the Canadian Army built the complex.

UNDERGROUND
ROADS AND HIGHWAYS

Massive engineering projects using huge tunneling machines have built underground transportation systems for cars and other vehicles.

Underground Down Under

The Cross City Tunnel in Sydney, Australia, is a 1.3-mile (2.1-km) long road tunnel. There is a tunnel for traffic going in each direction, and a third tunnel for ventilation. On most days, drivers can get from one side of the city to the other in around two minutes. Before the tunnel was built, the journey took more than 20 minutes.

A Very Big Dig

The Big Dig in Boston is an underground highway. Designed to replace a narrower elevated section of Interstate 90, the Big Dig took 15 years to build. More than 16 million cubic yards (12.2 million cubic meters) of soil were excavated and 3.8 million cubic yards (2.9 million cubic meters) of concrete were used.

The Cross City ▷
Tunnel in Sydney

Westbound tunnel

Into the Future

Elon Musk is a wealthy businessman and engineer. His **Boring** Company plans to build tunnels under Los Angeles. In the tunnels, electric transporters traveling up to 150 mph (240 km per hour) will carry cars. Pedestrian travelers will use cars designed for a number of people to travel through the tunnels.

△ Construction of the Interstate 90 tunnel connector in Boston

DID YOU KNOW?

In the future, Elon Musk's tunnels could also be used for the Hyperloop. This is a proposed high-speed rail system that will travel at up to 700 mph (1,126 kph).

Eastbound tunnel

Ventilation tunnel

BELOW LAND AND WATER

Some tunnels for trains have been built under huge mountains or below large stretches of water. There's even a tunnel being built in Norway that ships will sail through underground!

Trains under Mountains

The Gotthard Base Tunnel in Switzerland is the world's longest and deepest traffic tunnel. The two-tube tunnel opened in 2016 and is 35.5 miles (57 km) long. It took 17 years to build and cost $12 billion. The tunnel was dug by four huge machines, each one as long as four soccer fields. Around 28 million tons (25.4 million metric tons) of rock were **excavated**. Cargo trains also use the tunnel, and 40 million tons (36.3 million metric tons) of **freight** travel through it each year.

△ Trains traveling at 155 mph (250 kph) carry 15,000 passengers a day through the Gotthard Base Tunnel.

△ This train driver is doing a test run on the underground Liefkenshoek rail link.

Under Land and Water

The Liefkenshoek rail link runs beneath the Kanaal **Dock**, the Schelde River, and Waasland Canal in Antwerp in Belgium. The link has two tunnels beside each other and is 10 miles (16.2 km) long. The tunnels are 131 feet (40 m) under the river and 98 feet (30 m) under the canal's docks. The rail link can handle 109 freight trains every day traveling in each direction.

DID YOU KNOW?

The Stad Ship Tunnel is the world's first ship tunnel. due to be built beneath the Stad peninsula in Norway. Cruise liners. freight vessels. and smaller ships will all use the tunnel.

MINING TUNNELS

Underground mine tunnels help workers and equipment move on foot or tracks, and send material such as coal or gold to the surface. Mining tunnels are built in a similar way to road or rail tunnels.

Working Underground

In the past, miners often worked with shovels and picks, standing in water in flooded tunnels. In the early 1800s, some tunnels were so small that children had to work in the mines. They moved carts along the narrow tunnels. Animals were also used in mining. Horses that hauled wagons on the underground tracks were called pit ponies.

▽ In the 1800s, some tunnels were so small that even children could not stand upright.

The trapped miners at Copiapó (see below) were lifted to the surface one at a time in narrow steel rescue capsules.

DID YOU KNOW?

Mponeng in South Africa is the world's deepest gold mine. Its 236 miles (379 km) of tunnels are longer than the New York City Subway.

Danger in the Dark!

Mining has always been dangerous. In road and rail tunnels, the sides are made of concrete—designed to last for a long time. However, mining tunnels might only be needed for a few years. The sides may be lined with wood, which isn't as safe. **Cave-ins** still happen, sometimes even killing workers underground.

The Copiapó Accident

In 2010, there was a cave-in at a copper and gold mine in Copiapó, Chile. Thirty-three men were trapped 2,300 feet (700 m) underground and 3 miles (5 km) from the mine entrance. The miners were underground for 69 days before being rescued. Three large escape holes were drilled to where the miners were trapped.

THE CHANNEL TUNNEL

The Channel Tunnel is an incredible feat of engineering. Built between 1988 and 1994, it carries cargo trains, passenger trains, and a shuttle for road vehicles beneath the English Channel between the U.K. and France.

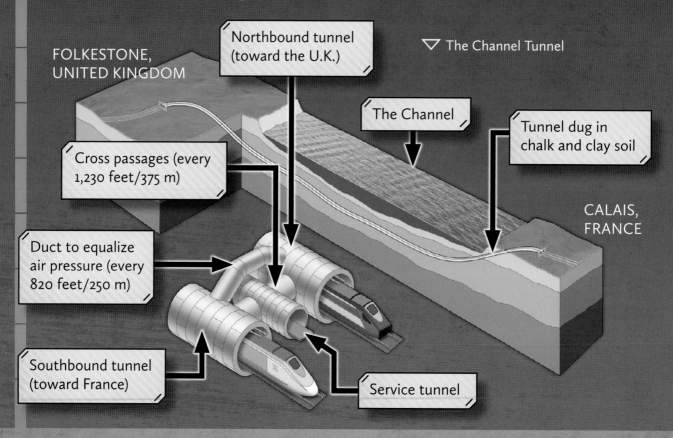

▽ The Channel Tunnel

FOLKESTONE, UNITED KINGDOM

Northbound tunnel (toward the U.K.)

The Channel

Tunnel dug in chalk and clay soil

Cross passages (every 1,230 feet/375 m)

Duct to equalize air pressure (every 820 feet/250 m)

CALAIS, FRANCE

Southbound tunnel (toward France)

Service tunnel

Meeting Challenges

Special boring machines were built that could cut through the chalky earth and withstand the great pressure on the seabed. The machines were also designed to collect the debris and move it behind them on conveyor belts. The tunnels were dug from both sides at the same time, so engineers used special measuring equipment to make sure they eventually met in the middle.

Safety under the Sea

Around 500 trains use the tunnel every day. There are two substations on each side of the tunnel. These supply electricity for the trains, lighting, and drainage pumps. If one substation is not working, the other can supply the whole system. There are also systems to detect fire in the tunnels.

△ Trains travel through the tunnel at speeds as high as 100 mph (160 kph), taking around 35 minutes to make the crossing.

DID YOU KNOW?

Eleven boring machines were used to build the tunnel. Each machine weighed around 450 tons (408 metric tons).

GLOSSARY

air raids Bombing campaigns against cities in wartime

Allied Describing countries that fought against Germany, Italy, and Japan in World War II

artificial reef An underwater structure that provides a habitat for marine life

barracks Buildings where soldiers or prisoners sleep in a camp

boring Making a hole in something

cave-in When a roof or wall collapses into a hollow area below, such as in a cave or mine

congestion Overcrowding

dock An enclosed area of water where ships load and unload cargo

excavated Hollowed out by digging

freight Things that are carried by a vessel or vehicle

gauge The distance between two rails on a track

investor Someone who gives money to help something get built

Middle Ages A period of history from about 500 to 1450 C.E.

mosaic A picture or design made up of small colored pieces of stone or tile

navigating Finding your way around

pioneering Describing something that has never been done before

Rock of Gibraltar A 2.6 square mile (6.7 square km) rocky outcrop on the coast of Spain

Russian Revolution The 1917 revolution that overthrew the Russian monarchy

sculpture A figure or design created in marble, clay, or metal

siege When a city, town, or fortress is surrounded by an army that is trying to capture it

token A piece of metal used instead of coins

turnstile A mechanical gate that lets people through it one at a time

ventilation A system that replaces stale air with fresh air

LEARNING MORE

Books

Durnin, Stephen, *London Underground Stations* (Capital Transport Publishing, 2010).

Donovan, Sandra, *The Channel Tunnel (Great Building Feats)* (Lerner, 2003).

Ponzi, Emilio, *The Great New York Subway Map* (Museum of Modern Art, 2018).

Websites

www.britannica.com/technology/subway

Learn more about the world's subway systems.

www.smithsonianmag.com/travel/secrets-new-york-city-subway-180958683/

Discover 12 secrets of the New York Subway.

www.eurotunnel.com/uk/build/

Learn how the Channel Tunnel was built.

INDEX

abandoned subway
  systems 16–17
accidents 10, 11, 27
art 11, 15

Big Dig 5, 22
bombs 8, 14
boring machines 28, 29

cave-ins 10, 27
Channel Tunnel 28–29
Cincinnati Subway 16–17
concrete 22, 27
congestion 4, 14
construction methods
  6, 10, 20
Cross City Tunnel 22

Dover Castle 18

electricity 4, 7, 29

freight trains 24, 25, 28

Gotthard Base Tunnel 24
Great Blizzard 10

hospitals 14, 18, 21
Hyperloop 23

Liefkenshoek rail link 25
London Underground
  6–9

mining tunnels 5, 26–27
mosaics 14, 15
Moscow Metro 14–15
Musk, Elon 23

New York City Subway
  4, 10–13, 27

rail systems 4, 6–9,
  10–13, 14–15, 24–25
rivers 4, 7, 14
road tunnels 22–23, 28
Rock of Gibraltar 20–21
Roosevelt, Franklin D. 17

Russian Revolution 14

sculptures 11, 15
secret tunnels 5, 18–19,
  20, 21
Stad Ship Tunnel 25
Stalag Luft III 19
Stalin, Joseph 14
stations 7, 8, 9, 13, 14, 15,
  16, 17
steam trains 7

Thames Tunnel 7
tickets 12
tokens 12
tracks 4, 6, 16, 17
tunneling shield 14
turnstiles 12

ventilation 5, 22, 23

World War II 8, 17, 18, 19